Dedicated

to Alexis and Hannah who inspired this book.
It is so fun to watch you grow into the women you are becoming and we hope you are never afraid to chase your passions. And to our new Finley who was the perfect addition to the family. Mommy and Daddy are so proud of each of you and can't wait to see what you grow into.

Why do Mommy and Daddy work?

Daddy wakes up every morning and gets ready for work.
He leaves every day with his briefcase.

Mommy seems to work all of the time. Every time she is on the phone, I have to sit in the other room and stay quiet.

Why do Mommy and Daddy work?

They say it's to make money for our family, but what do we need the money for?

Mommy decided to stay home from work one day to show me.

First, we went to the grocery store. We bought bread, milk, and eggs. Since I was so good, Mommy bought me gummies for a treat!

When it was our turn in line, Mommy opened her purse and gave the cashier money.

We work so we can eat.

After that, Mommy said we needed to get gas for our car. Our car won't go anywhere without gas.

When she was done, Mommy had to pay for the gas.

We work so we can go places.

Once we had gas, Mommy took me shopping.
Winter time was coming and I was growing so big, I didn't
have any coats that fit me.

I tried on a beautiful pink coat with purple buttons and big pockets. Mommy said I could wear it since I loved it so much, but we had to pay for it first!

We work so we can have warm clothes.

When we left the store, we saw a man outside ringing a bell. Mommy took some money from her purse and put it in his bucket. She said his job is to collect money for those who have no money for food or clothes.

We work so we can give.

After a long day, we came back to our warm home. I turned on the lights and left the room. Mommy told me to come back and, "Turn off those lights, please."

She explained that using the lights costs money, and they should not be on if we are not using them.

We work so we can turn on lights.

When Daddy came home, I ran to him, jumped into his arms, and gave him a big hug! When he put me down, I took his hand.

Thank you for working, Daddy! I didn't know
we had to pay for so many things!

When Mommy and Daddy tucked me into bed that night, I asked them, "Is money important?"

"Oh no," they said, "you are important!"

"We use the money to take care of you. We love you so much, we want to make sure you have good food to eat, clothes to keep you warm, and most of all...

... you will give to others
all that you are able."

CPSIA information can be obtained
at www.ICGtesting.com
Printed in the USA
LVHW010251220619
622063LV00017B/436/P